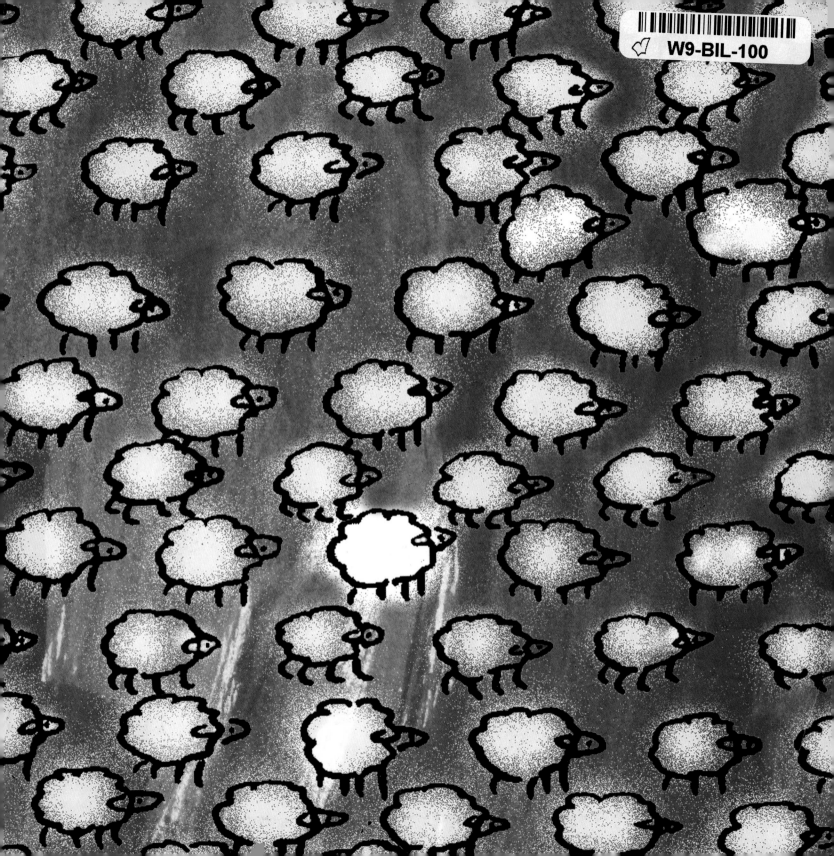

One
Lost Sheep

RHONDA GOWLER GREENE
PICTURES BY
SANTIAGO COHEN

zonderkidz.
The children's group
of Zondervan

www.zonderkidz.com

One Lost Sheep
Copyright © 2007 by Rhonda Gowler Greene
Illustrations © 2007 by Santiago Cohen

Requests for information should be addressed to:
Grand Rapids, Michigan 49530

Library of Congress Cataloging-in-Publication Data
Greene, Rhonda Gowler.
  One lost sheep / by Rhonda Gowler Greene.
    p. cm.
  ISBN-13: 978-0-310-71098-1 (printed hardcover)
  ISBN-10: 0-310-71098-7 (printed hardcover) 1. Lost sheep (Parable)-Juvenile
literature. I. Title.
  BT378.L6G74 2007
  226.8'09505-dc22

                              2006005637

Editor: Amy De Vries
Interior design: Al Cetta

Printed in China

07 08 09 10 11 • 10 9 8 7 6 5 4 3 2 1

Then Jesus told them this parable:
"Suppose one of you has a hundred sheep and loses one of them. Does he not leave the
ninety-nine in the open country and go after the lost sheep until he finds it?"
Taken from Luke 15:3-4

For my son, Matt, with love—RGG

To my sister Ruth, my favorite sheep—PA'

White and wooly,
hungry sheep
grazing by a mountain, steep.

Shepherd watching
them with care,
guards each one from beast and bear.

Counts to make sure all are there…

One, two,
three, four,
five, six, even more…

Big ones, small ones,
ewes and rams,
brothers, sisters, little lambs…

...ninety-eight,
ninety-nine,
one hundred sheep.
Yes, all are fine.

Shepherd leads
his flock of sheep
to clear, cool stream past mountain, steep.

Down the path
clip-clop they go,
stepping sure, stepping slow.

Uh-oh! One
begins to stray.
Little lamb, don't lose your way!

Clip…clop
up mountain, steep.
*Baa…Baa…*one lost sheep.

Now Shepherd counts
just ninety-nine.
One lost sheep,
  he must find!

Step, step, step
up mountain, steep.
Where, oh where,
  is that lost sheep?

In the brambles?
No, not there.
Searching,
      searching everywhere…

Behind those rocks?
No, not there.
Searching,
    searching everywhere…

Listen…Shhh…
That wayward lamb
bleating *baa baa* here I am.

Shepherd lifts
that sheep up high,
rejoices
    with a happy sigh.

Carries it
down mountain, steep,
safe and sound now in his keep.

Shares his gladness
all around, tells his friends his sheep is found.

White and wooly,
sleepy sheep
dozing by a mountain, steep.

Shepherd watching
through the night
as the stars shine brilliant-bright.

Like that shepherd, God above
keeps us in his boundless love.

The Lord God is our shepherd too,
watching over...
   me and you.

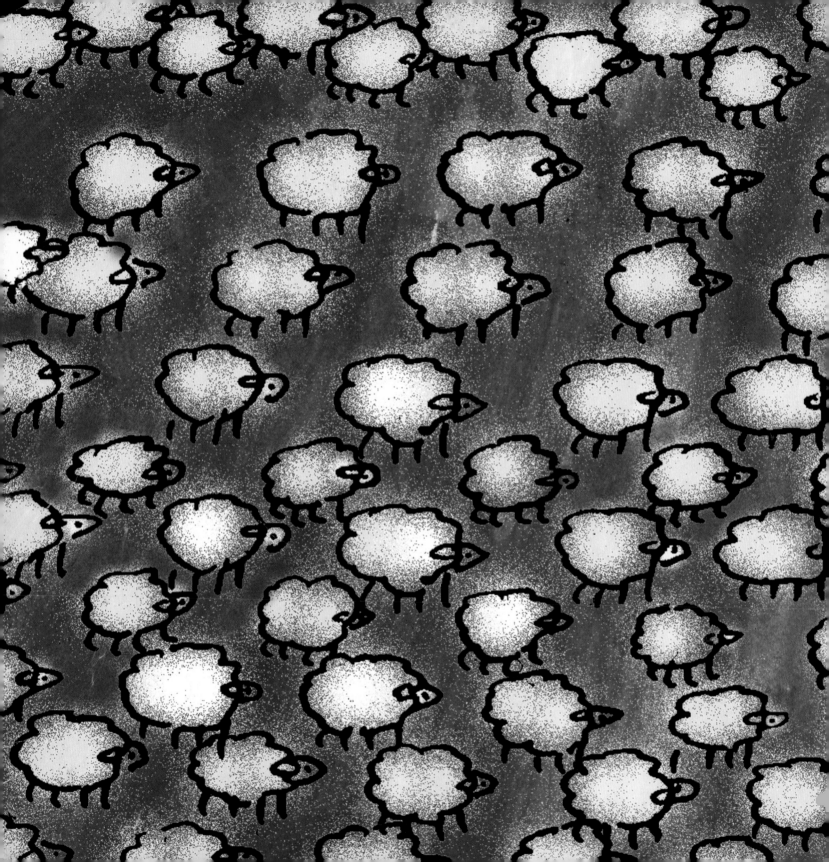